LYONESSE

ACKNOWLEDGEMENTS

Acknowledgements are due to the editors of the following publications in which some of these poems first appeared:

Lyonesse: *Aquanauts* (Sidekick Books), *And Other Poems, Arfur, Artemis, The Broadsheet, The Beach Hut, finished creatures, Ink, Sweat and Tears, The Manhattan Review, The Long Poem Magazine, Poetry and all that Jazz, Poetry Salzburg,* and *Under the Radar.*

Four poems appeared as a mini-pamphlet from Stickleback (Hedgehog Press)

My thanks to the Authors' Foundation for a grant which enabled me to work on this collection.

New Lamps for Old: *Artemis, The Broadsheet, finished creatures, Poetry London, Raceme,* and *Reliquiae.*

CONTENTS

NEW LAMPS FOR OLD

PREFACE

'The gownshops of Lyonesse took satin for granted...'

This first line came into my head out of nowhere one day in January 2015 while I was walking in Cornish drizzle at Trebah Gardens. I sat down and wrote a poem about *Lyonesse*. The remainder of the collection followed, in serial batches, over the next eighteen months in a spontaneous inundation of approaches to the theme, images, soundings of *Lyonesse*. I also drew on memories of a visit to the Isles of Scilly in 2013. We flew there from Land's End airport in an eight-seater plane. To see the Isles from above, at low altitude, and to fly over the Wolf Lighthouse were key to the writing. Both imagination and memory played their part in joining the Lyonesse dots together. Having the first drafts I then spent a considerable time shaping the poems. The poems began with pure feeling, but my editing process employed various poetic strategies concerning form, architecture, the colour palette, and finding a balance, a pathway between mystery and clarity. I also wove some quotes from Lyonesse poems by authors such as Thomas Hardy, Walter de la Mare, David Jones and Marianne Moore into the text.

Why *Lyonesse*? I have lived in Cornwall all my adult life, and *Lyonesse* is an alternative if sometimes 'tourist-friendly' handle for Cornwall. The name goes back a long way. Hardy used it, famously. The story of this submerged region comes to us through myth and the oral tradition, often standing for a lost paradise.

Lyonesse might stand also as an example of human frailty in the face of climate change. Scientific evidence confirms that a Bronze Age inundation swept the entire west of Cornwall under the sea, with only the Isles of Scilly and St Michael's Mount left as remnants above the tide level.

In November 2015 the exhibition *Sunken Cities* opened at the British Museum. This exhibition displayed ancient objects, statues of gods and other mythic figures, recovered from the seabed from the submerged Egyptian cities of Thonis-Heracleion and Canopus, great trading and cultural centres of their day. Seeing these archaic objects of great beauty and intense feeling brought further energising and exhilarating material into the compass of Lyonesse. The universality of loss, both of physical cities and of the human experience erased from the record, enhanced the resource of this undersea city in my writing. Lyonesse is a place of paradox. It is real, had historical existence. It is also an imaginary region for exploring depths. It holds grief for many kinds of loss. A poetics that explores the oceanic, riches found on the seabed, will also be an exploration of the riches to be found in the collective unconscious. This territory offers us renewal and deep engagement with our fullest selves, essential at all times but perhaps never more so than at the present moment when huge threats face our vulnerable planet.

John Keats, in his *Endymion, Book III*, portrays Neptune's kingdom.

> Far as the mariner on highest mast
> Can see all round upon the calmed vast,
> So wide was Neptune's hall: and as the blue
> Doth vault the waters, so the waters drew
> Their doming curtains, high, magnificent,
> Aw'd from the throne aloof; – and when storm-rent
> Disclos'd the thunder-gloomings in Jove's air...

My *Lyonesse* is Neptune's Hall, where what has been lost becomes golden in memory. But that gold must be scrutinised, weighed. *Lyonesse* has its dark places but also possesses milder regions where, for instance, puns on lions mediate the starker areas of loss. The poems seek the re-wilding of a city where human loss interconnects with mythic loss; myth is rooted in the real. In Adrienne Rich's famous lines it is –

the thing I came for:
the wreck and not the story of the wreck
the thing itself and not the myth...

Out of Cornish drizzle *Lyonesse* offered me new ways to write about loss. It became a sub-aquatic rite of passage. I explored the allure of the past, the vanities of the present, the perils of the future. I sought to hold on to the sense that 'nothing is ever truly lost'. The undersea city gained, in Jung's phrase, 'psychic actuality'. Language is a serious and yet playful affair. Visiting *Lyonesse* can teach us how not to be drowned in melancholy, to take the measure of loss, to manage and learn from inundations of feeling. I had both delight and sorrow in mapping *Lyonesse*.

At key moments in this process I came up for air from the watery depths of *Lyonesse*. I began writing non-*Lyonesse* poems, to re-tune my senses. The poems in *New Lamps for Old* – the second part of this book – are an account of finding ways to begin again, to find meaning in life after bereavement. The 'old lamps' of a former life have been extinguished, leaving darkness. The challenge is to find 'new lamps' to illuminate and give meaning to life.

Both collections explore the paradoxical. 'Hurry up, says the tortoise.'

Lyonesse is a fluid magical world. The poems of *New Lamps for Old* are concerned with earth, air and fire. Both collections share allegiance with the fifth element, the spirit.

In his essay *Alchemical Blue and the Unio Mentalis*, James Hillman says, 'The blue transit between black and white is like that sadness which emerges from despair and proceeds towards reflection.' The poems of *New Lamps* almost all began with a transit from sadness, moving via reflection in language to (it is my hope) poems possessing energised repose. Life, which was not interesting because of sadness, became interesting when new illuminations came along. The poems were written not by concentrated acts but by everyday openness to life in my post-bereavement solitude. They track and trace where I went, what I felt, how I led a widowed life, tried to make sense of it, find purpose.

The *New Lamp* poems focus on memory, glances over the shoulder, sidelong glimpses. Light is shed on to the dark memory of time spent in the hellish zone of deep grief and holds that anguish in a fresh regard, enabling the alleviation of pain, a letting go. New aspects of illumination change everything. Poetry releases us into our own custody. I was often surprised as I wrote by the rapid transitions from sadness to a lightening of the spirit. Looking back or being in the inescapable now both bring danger, but we move from stasis towards possibility.

Can poetry 'seal wounds with love'. I think it can, whether we are reader or writer.

'Why poetry?' asks Robert Creeley. 'Its materials are so constant, simple, elusive, specific. It costs so little and so much. It preoccupies a life, yet can only find one in living. It is music, a playful construct of feeling, a last word and a communion.' Both *Lyonesse* and *New Lamps for Old* were written employing processes very much in the sphere and spirit of Creeley's words.

PENELOPE SHUTTLE

LYONESSE

(Back over

        the drowned tillage of Leonnoys

        over the smothered defences

over the one hundred and forty *mensae* drowned

in the un-apsed *eglwysau*, under.

Back to the crag mound

        in the drowned *coed*

        under.)

DAVID JONES
from *The Anathemata*

                *

slant-lit green
at the bottom of a field

we are under
neath

summer's growth for us floods a
Lea-on-Ness

MARK GOODWIN
from *a St Juliot, Steps*

Door

I opened a door   found myself in a city under the sea
where everyone knew me by name
and no one thought it a problem to go with the flow
breathing salt water instead of air   I must be in heaven (I said)
but a woman murmured   no   you're in Lyonesse

Palm Sunday

When the wave
hit Lyonesse
with a run-up height of
over forty metres
it sealed the churches full of people
stoppered them up with five million tons of fatal debris
Side-swiped orchards crashed down
to the abyssal plain
no longer dependent upon the sun
Repair garages sparked like broken wineglasses at a wedding

The hands of the planet could not lift a finger to help

They say the tilt-yards of Lyonesse
took to shamanism
They say a cooked goose was waiting
in every oven
in that gobsmack city of the dead
They say
the tremblor of the event
shortened the length
of the world's day by a microsecond
They say fjords a thousand miles away sloshed in seismic sympathy
They say icebergs broke off
the Sulzberger Ice Shelf in Antarctica
All this is true

The Gownshops

of Lyonesse
took satin for granted, silk
was cheaper than salt,
but velvet rip-roared
like *the water-lions of the west*
who dealt the city its fate

Those frocks wore themselves
to rags overnight
along streets pinned to the tides,
gardens groomed by the waves

When the weather
forgot its place in Lyonesse,
every dress was a flounce
in the wrong direction
in all the bars and ballrooms
as the city swam for its life

And in the last wet mirror
Lyonesse held up to itself,
not a gown to be seen,
nor a child,
if tempest-truth be told,
in the place where Lyonesse had been

Our Cradle Sea

the sleepers turn their faces
to the west
the beech trees
bear fruit every autumn
and the forest you could see
from the city gate
still waits for the huntsmen
though only bream
gurnard and monkfish
slip through
the branches of oak and ash
in the green ocean
where no living person
can remain
lully lullay

Strike, strike the bell

Backalong
we named our lasses
not from bible maids
but after the good boats
bobbing out on the tide
      Wavelette
      Rosanna
      Nancy-Belle
gals and trawlers
long gone
where now the white beluga
breathe the four winds of ocean
and remember the slain

Make a Wish

The sky has no favourites in Lyonesse
but favours all with its fair or foul
Lyonesse will always be
just what you want it to be
streets paved
with the sea

days of dogfish and dolphin
the swordfish patrolling
aisle and pew
nights learning their place
in rockpool after rockpool

Lyonesse offers you
what can't be given or taken
bought or sold
here you can have everything
you wish for   and wish for
and wish it away
as Lyonesse goes down in the sigh of the last ship

Kelpy

nettles of the neighbourhood
sank down
rain was strewn for miles
the storm lasted seven days
and seven nights
flinging down matted maps
of the sodden heavens
it smelt
rocky and kelpy
its kraken roar rattled Lyonesse
like Rodin sorting through
his drawer of Legs and Hands –
then
       Zut!
away went the storm to wherever storms go
for a change of scene
flinging back its bushy cloud hair
its *cheveux touffus*
leaving that ole home town
no better no worse
than a wishing well of weather

easy

but it's easy
to gather up the frescoes
silver altars
and string quartets
of Léonois
along with the palazzos
and old Alfa Romeos
plazas and boathouses
a hard thing to do
with London or New York
but here everything
squinches down small enough
for folding
autumn and winter
squeezing in
at the last moment
and the Dalmatian horse
yes everyone make room
for the black and white horse
quick before the sea rises
quick before I tuck
tiny folded-up Lyonesse
into my pocket for safe-keeping

Inscribed on a Stela found on the seabed

down here
no one cares
if you're honest or a liar
rich or poor
the only virtue here
is how much
you've forgotten
of that blood-boltered world
above the shiver
and pound
of the waves
you must forget everything
says Lyonesse
everything but
down
here

Sentimental Customs

Their patron saint wasn't Saint Piran
or Saint George
or even Saint Bride
she of the light's blessing
but flower-crowned Mister Valentine

Lyonesse was a city of lovers

I've seen his reputed skull
in a golden casket in Rome
but who can tell
one martyr's bonce from another?

A small reliquary
tinged with his blood
moseys along the tideline
blessing the sea to this very day
long after the *will-you-be-my...* lovers
are plentiful bone on the seabed

Night Gate

Lyonesse sleeps
by the night gate

by the shore folded round
by a muddle of mud

by slicks and currents
by the bridge and by the wharf

Lyonesse sleeps
in its council house heap

all the forty-wink night
all night by the nightful

under the fantail sky
under the church's look

you know the way it stares
long and hard as we go by

by the hoar rock in the drowned wood

there was once
a feasting-cup city

pearl and aquamarine
of its precincts and palaces

sea-green peridot
of its square miles

but no one knows a way back
through time

to when Lyonesse
was fresh from the hands of its makers

No one can bear to think
of its libraries

given to or snatched up
by the sea,

illuminated missals,
neatly-kept annals,

mathematical and philosophical treatises
of its thinkers,

rare volumes swollen
and blotched beyond rescue

Are its people lost
in the sullen courts of sleep

or are they listening even now
for the approach

of the first responders,
hoping to be ferried to safety,

not daring to look back at
roofs, walls, belfries of the foundered town?

here's my Lyonesse

        back from olden times

she's been far away

        while many leaves fell

many moons went west

      and the SS *Blue Jacket*

        sailed over the edge of the world

Legends

The lions of Lyonesse
were legends
in their own raw lunchtime

If a lion might swagger past you
or bask
all afternoon in your courtyard

you'd look the other way
show respect –
no child of the city
ever play-roared back at a lion

Day and night
their meat-breath mocked the city

No salt-sharp air
no sea-garden lavender after rain
sweetened
that ravenous pong

The *lewyon* of Lionville
knew their place
no one   and nothing above them

those golden guys with manes
and gaping slavering jaws
the piss-backward lords of Lyonesse

Fortuna

I'm swimming
the flood-streets
shuffling salt-stained
cards of my tarot
as the white storm
bares its teeth
and the billowing houses
shrink to sea-chest ruins

I'm swimming streets ahead
of drowning Lyonesse
whose vestals
are reaping the whirlwind I predicted,
whose widows cast the first stone to this very day

Owls

The owls of Lyonesse
found themselves blown
feather beak and claw
and St Hilary
can see
when the city
and the white horses

those clever fowl
clean inland
as far as St Paul
as far as a Penwith eye
on that fateful night
swam for its life
went galloping sky-high

Now on calm nights
on the sea floor
as the owls fly round
they fly around
his lank shadow

you can hear their hooves
quiet as your heartbeat
The Wolf
The Wolf
slinking across Lethowstow

clad me naked

from the coffers of Lyonesse
  a weather wringing its hands

from the tongue of Lyonesse
  silence billing and cooing

from Lyonesse as she was and is
  everything you could possibly ask for

an empty hopechest
  a hornpipe a fingerbone

Why the Maidens prefer future funk to a Sumerian goat

The maidens accidentally killed by Apollo
poor wee hens

have gone to Lyonesse to learn
about the afterlife

setting sail in a flotilla of girl-talk
greeting the elf-queen at the dock

The maidens slain by Apollo
young god of plague and sunlight

so beautiful when he fought at Troy
are revving it up to the max

go go go ma fine wee hens!

    Let his Lordship shine
        brighter than all the suns!
    Let him devour Troy in a single bite
        like it was brunch!

    Let it rock   let it roll
        we don' wan'
        we don' wan'
        we don' wan' no gods at all

Interviewing Neptune

Sire, are you tired of the taste of salt,
the burden of ships?

No comment

Are you drawn to the dry land,
or does it leave you cold, Sire?

No comment

Do you plan to retire, Oceanus,
to your own place in the sun?
And also, Majesty,
what is your opinion of rivers?

No comment

Some words of advice or comfort
for the drowned, the buried-at-sea, Lord?

No comment

Do you, by and large, Sire,
see eye to eye with The Moon,
or regard her as rival,
She who owns the tides?

The Moon?
(A stormy snort). *That amateur!*

Shall I put that down as *no comment*, Sire?

My Friend

Sometimes I glimpse my friend
glinting beneath
the shape-shift silvers
of the waves
I don't know how she got down there
so near and so far from the blessed isles nor how long she'll stay
but there she is
      fathoms deep
pacing the boulevards of Lyonesse
searching each *casement and porch*
of water-wounded temple and storm-shattered fane
hauling her sorrow through the coral crossways
She isn't alone   my friend
Others while away the long hours
treading alley and ope of that *green translucency*
looking for the ones   who will never be found
down there in a city laid-out   in its own legend

In the dark

Lyonesse can't get used to the darkness
though it's all there is to see by.
The Mayor orders a dozen morning suns
but they always never arrive.

Somewhere things are different.
Windows are drunk on light.
Noonday glitters
over miles of roads and beautiful nettles.
Light sheers off a silver Dreamliner.

Lyonesse can't get used to the dark.
You'd think there'd be a switch,
a candle, a match. Nada, natch.
Light's moving finger writes its word,
but not for this city, never for her.

Saturdays & Sundays

Remember our Lyonesse Saturdays,
queuing for bread and milk?
And on blameless Sundays we'd visit
what you called: our parlour in the pines.
I think we were happy nine-tenths of the time.
Then you travelled to where whales
are never watched, leaving me the small change
of my spare time, endless coppery Saturdays
and silver Sundays. I learned how our days
are numbered and how years go by.

Last summer I heard of a woman in London
who was ready and willing to die.
But the day she'd chosen went by without taking her.
Weekend after weekend, she wondered   *why?*

When the Devil seals the seam with hot pitch

there's no more sleep for anyone
the silence everywhere at 3.17 am precisely
singing out its saltwater hymnal
along the woken street
where a moving finger's *tekel upharsin*
goes unread because in the middle of the night
you can't remember how to read
as you bound
from wide-awake house to house
past street-corner tabernacle and childbirth museum
peering in a spindrift window
looking for a companion to join you
in celebrating the city's plethora of lions
busy all night translating the bible
the Song of Songs to be precise

into their own belly and fang idiom

Midsummer:

    the children of Lyonesse

        offer rainwater

            to the city's parched lips

Lizzie

Way down
at the bottom of the sea
Lizzie Siddal is plaiting her claret-red hair

Her beggar-maid's glance shifts here and there
in the smooth-as-swansdown   smooth-as-a-baby's-bottom light
and the light in its turn brushes her...

I know the sea is never quieter
than when it speaks to me like a mighty uncle
says Lizzie   but why does that deep blue voice never flirt with me?

Down here I like to sing in the high and the low of my tongue
and who knows how many lovers
I'll meet in the stepping-high lanes of the sea
pouts dear Lizzie
naughty anchorite   at home in sea-lost Lyonesse

Willow o' the Wisp

Lyonesse
undoes the field
like a gate
slips in under the willows
like fate

Along the quiet path
up the silent stair
Lyonesse
is here
is there

Take care
take care

Holy Father Lions

Around Cape Horn   there's ice and snow
but lions know   where not to go

Holy Father Lions   bigwigs   celebs
gold chains   looped in their manes

Around Cape Horn   there's ice and snow
but lions know   where not to go

they like mauling   treasure chests
licking shrimp   off dead men's vests

Around Cape Horn   there's ice and snow
but lions know   where not to go

Lions never sail   on the Sweet Trinity
they don't do   shipwreck

Around Cape Horn   there's ice and snow
but lions know   where not to go

Lions prowl –   growling all through
the second year   of seabed fieldwork

disliking more   than they can roar
the *squeak/ mouse/ squeak*   of the scientific sonar

hunting for hints   of Leonoys

O Shake That Girl with the Blue Dress On

I'll be your *partner in fainting*
I'll fly out of the storm's eye
be your sword blade
in the hard school of blood
I'll lift the leaden weight
of your tongue,
leopard all your lions
I'll eye-spy you in the bobbing shadow
the coastguard 'copter casts
on the deep blue sea
and in the solitudes of the week
after half-term
I'll bring you my bird-in-the-hand
pitch you the swansong of Lyonesse

Boat-drawn

Not a word I say
counts
in this boat-drawn city
where no one cares
if I live or die
which is good for me
to take on board
the world does not revolve
around me
as I was often told as a child
nor does it owe me a cent
and in this full-blown boat-drawn city
I can only murmur from street to street
how true   Lyonesse   how true

Rusalka

I'm not in tears   dear me no
though the cloven hoof of my heart
begs to differ

I'm just a party girl
you threw overboard
from your drunken boat

the girl who's to blame for everything

Siren Scholarship

tells us
> a few sirens
>> were given passage
>>> on Noah's Ark
>>>> but history has mislaid them
>>>>> those midday songsters
>>>>>> warbling magic songs
>>>>>>> to any passing mariner
>>>>>>>> and shedding tears
>>>>>>>>> the Mock Turtle
>>>>>>>>>> would envy

The Foster Brothers of Kernow Speak

Lady Lyonesse thinks igh of erself
biggin up
her beauty   n such

Runnin into us ole boyos
she can't elp boosting er tits
n banterin   givin' us the eye

But she'm tricksy
Just when you thinks
she gonna lap youse up

she be gone   leavin you
in the heartbroke dark
          eh bro?

Sewing Lesson under the Sea

Cut and piece a marriage quilt
from your bloke's raised fist.

Work his taunts and his belt
into its drunken-path pattern.

Add the quick of evening,
midday's logic, every she-wolf dawn.

Birds-in-the-air.
Windblown square.

Stretch the bruise-black fabric
over the birch wood frame.

Say your wishes, one, two, three.
This quilt will be the making of you.

land under sea

tir o dan y môr

luz azpian itsasoa

terram sub mari

merram alla

terra sob o mar

taħt sath il-baħar

ile labe okun

lân ûndersee

An Account of the Submergence

Now that we have wiped Lyonesse from the Departures Board (the starry way to Lyonesse no longer valid) let us record what we know so far. When Lyonesse saw daylight, the harbour blew its own trumpet. Everyone is agreed on that. Great ships sailed the roadstead, their shadows keeping close by, like rose gardens. Streets went about in their mischief. A hundred churches stood at the right hand of the swordsman. Even in Lyonesse a sword had to wash its blade free of the caked gore.

We know moreover that at a date and time not yet confirmed, Lyonesse lost her grip on plash of air and earth's wishbone. Lyonesse the lovely fell to her knees, but kept knitting seaweed shawls for her newborns. Lyonesse had been on her deathbed for a very long time before the Inundation Event drove her out of Europe, the shark's toothcomb parting the waves above her ruin.

And what of the other cities of the submergence, Ravenser Odd which knew *A Great Drowning of Men*, Doggerland, Is, Zealandia, super-rich celebrity-resort Baiae, all spooling away in somersault schools of spinner dolphin...

It was Mission Impossible for Lyonesse. The birds shoved off. Dogs rolled their eyes, cats counted their lives. The Wave-Dragon lashed his tidal tail and the four winds ran amuck. Teacup and storm could not agree. Mirror and reflection went their separate ways, as the lion city flinched back from the slap of fate across its civic cheek.

The submergence shattered mirrors, snapped staircases in two. It made star-shaped cracks in brick and metal. The sea dealt the deathblow like a scatterbrain, punching the hieroglyph for drowning into the city's solar plexus. One thousand and one bedrooms, drowned. Glimmery Bourse and crystalline Parliament, drowned. Even the rococo-style abattoirs. Gone.

This most fleet-footed of cities (says an eyewitness) dipped down into the sea in a matter of minutes, went down boxing the compass full fathom five...headfirst among porpoise and white lobster, man o'war jellyfish and narwhal. Lyonesse belly-flopped past wreck and deadman's chest, seismic arms clenched round her marvels until the undersea city was a scuttle of amber rooms... Yet was the city (asks the eye-witness) a willing sacrifice, crashing down to rest on the murky seabed?

What can we learn from this? That water paid its last respects to Lyonesse, to the endlands of Cornwall, or was it Normandy, or Brittany? That Lyonesse went down with all hands, dovecotes awash, politicians and scholars maintaining to the very last moment that the situation 'is something we can deal with'? Let us assume the terrible rising of the waters taught believers and unbelievers alike to know fear at last. Even the diamonds in the women's ears regretted their watermarks as the waters, fresh and salt, holy and brackish, surged higher and higher...

If any living hand, says an expert, knew how to hold back the sea or dangle an ocean by its tail, it was not found in Lyonesse.

We've been here before. Ten thousand kingdoms have fanned out their empires then faded, as history demands. Some were last-breathed by plague. Others trampled under barbarian hooves. Some were carbonised by pyroclastic surge, as at Herculaneum. Others died of simple thirst, famine.

Let us imagine what sport the waves make today along those streets and boulevards. The sea has the city all to itself. There it is, hidden in the tide's corner, the quiet's ear. Shoals of blue whiting tingle here and there as one, and the great sharks promise the diver nothing but harm. Miles overhead a trawler shimmers darkly along as, perhaps, many eyes look up from the struck-dumb seabed theatres. No one knows. But Léonois turns over in our sleep, wondering what will become of us.

Our conclusion is that the seas will go on rising. That cities not yet destroyed will turn blind eye and deaf ear to Lyonesse the wiser.

land under sea
tierra bajo el mar
pozemok pod morom
land undir sjó
pansi pa nyanja
whenua i raro i te moana
mark under havet
terre sous mer
peyi anba lanmè

Church of the Crayfish Christ

Someone is singing
by leaps and bounds
on her happy way
to church
in the parish of Lyonesse
where men and women cling
to the helping hands of music
and when Our Lord the Crayfish Christ
sings out his sermon
to our listening ears
we the congregation understand
everything for the very first time

Beloveds
you must live for pleasure alone!
This is my gospel
Am I not half-brother to the moon?
Are not the deeds of my claw everlasting joy and delight?

Alleluia and Amen
Praise to the Crayfish Christ Our King!

Up jumps the shark

with his nine rows of teeth:
>the harp folds its wings
>>the birds become strangers to Lyonesse

Up jumps the eel with his slippery tail:
>zigzagging holy fool
>>with no kind word for Lyonesse

Up jumps the lobster with his mighty claw:
>the hothead's elected to office
>>forest and marshland are no longer green kinsmen
>>>the sooth-saw casts her last spell

Up jumps the whale, vastest of all:
>we've lived hard times since he put the deluge to bed boys
>>hard times all round on Holy Ground
>>>on Holy Holy Ground

Starlit

If Lyonesse
was on the map
you'd go there this very minute
but Leonoys
keeps everyone guessing

The man or woman
you've loved
all these years
without rhyme or reason
put 'im in the long boat
put 'er in the long boat
is the only one who knows
the starlit way to Lyonesse
and he or she
is always out of reach
like Lethowstow
       Léonois
           Leonoys
               Lyonaise

On St Mary's Quayside an old salt button-holes a passer-by

…there's no one style of pirate ship, pal, sloop or ship-of-the-line,
we use any brig we can get our hands on.
It must be fast though. The pirate code forbids me to tell you more.

Years spent in jail gave me a high regard for iron,
master of power, structure, suspension, brutality.
An iron shirt never needs ironing.

Nowadays I like the air better…salty up-draughts and thermals,
clouds like sky-cloaked widow-women carrying harps of hornbeam and brass,
busy with their Acts of Pardon and Acts of Grace.

My fine ship *The Lyonesse* has a compass for all weathers,
she's been blessed, she's goose-winged and trim.
Paso a bordo, amigo. Out of harbour we'll hoist the jolly blood-red flag,
I'll read aloud from the West Briton to comfort you as we speed the flashing
brine.

Many brave hearts are asleep in the deep, so beware, beware

The sea casts new bells for Lyonesse
out of the debris of lobster carcass

wriggle-writhe of conger eel
everyday sandgrains and shells

and out of the great iron ships
rendered down to odds and ends
by The Synod of the tides

The sea hoist-drags the bells along
one by one to the 140 fallen belfries

hangs them horizontal
taps them with its real-time currents

strumming out a zithery bell-song
for those who care to listen...

Jackie Onassis orders new dancing shoes,

cost-the-earth shoes fashioned from sealskin,
        bearskin, mouse-skin,
                lion-pelt,

peep-toes, sling-backs and stilettos
        flashy with ibis and eagle wing,
                raven and snow bunting,

gold-crest and wren feather,
        satin pumps white as January in the north,
                tap shoes of broken glass

Her shoemaker can make shoes out of anything
        here in Lyonesse
                But Jackie won't dance   no

She stashes them
        in her walk-in closet big as an aircraft hanger
                How sad to hear her sighing in there

                        now she's left her dancing days air-side

Twinned with Canopus

Did the gods grieve
when Canopus and Lyonesse
were wiped from the face of the earth
or did they say
What fools these mortals be?
Gold-eyed Osiris watching
from his funerary lion-shaped bed
and Alexander himself
couldn't save those cities
famed for their courtesans
and their religious tolerance
the part they played in stocking the warehouses of ancient Egypt

They say the voiced angel is an invention of the English

I'd like to live in an attic room
high above the harbour

I'd watch Brythonic confusions of weather
draw veils over loopholes in the sky

I'd like to live in god-forsaken Lyonesse
changing my mind about everything   whenever I please

There are blood red roses in Lyonesse   all the hours I'll ever need
Sometimes thunder   making me feel safe   held in the hummable furry
fist of a storm-bee

More deadly than the Siren's song is the Siren's silence

Our rock-throned post-Homeric Siren
sings the story of her childhood
honest in nothing but the christening

She does this to please no one
not even her sister Mrs Do-As-You-Would-Be-Done-By
down where the waves turn tail and turtle
bringing us no good news at all

Fifteen gold doubloons swish
through her restless hand
and when she falls silent
how can we not listen forever?

We are the servants of lions

Lyonesse
is made of voices
so you can't hear yourself think
no matter how quietly
they're speaking
you don't want to know
what they're saying anyway
those voices mean business
and now there's a door
in the walled-up air
where you find yourself entering
there's no smile here at all
though there are
of course
the voices

Sea Street

Half the street's
in shadow

Half's bright and angry
as daytime telly

Chartered street
where a couple of shillings

will buy you
a brief delight

or maybe not
darlin'

Where the storyteller offers you
his favourite silence

and the lion-house lays
its iron lips against yours

The Restorer

To renew
the washed-out colours
of Lyonesse
he uses a palette
gorgeous with wine and woe
his brush
staving off the elements

He works faster
than an offshore wind farm
in a force ten
and when he grasps the nettle of me
I'm tear-honed
tongued-tied
just the way I like it

May the Holy Ghost blow your sailboat home

Lyonesse is not half sister
to the sea for nothing

nor is her gap year
spent working a blue-mist farm

Lyonesse is a blind alley
where I forget

what hangs my bones together
because when all's said and done

I'm no more
than that line on a weather map

inked-in more darkly to show
rain is here

The Devil

In Lyonesse
the Devil is still an Englishman
speaking English
to all his Luciferian angels
(and not some skanky language
fit only for lions)
as the bards frown in Cornish
and the sailors off Land's End draw up nets
crammed with old doors   *casements and porches*
from the place they call *The Town*

I've seen for myself a Lyonesse
made of ice and air
and sunshine
conjured on a blue winter sea in Falmouth Bay –
polychrome towers, medallioned piers,
portals, spires and porticoes,
columns mimicking trees and branches,
hierophantic clusters
of maypole belfries,
courtier-like and gaudy for god,
all the ruthless architectural audacity
and curvaceous elaboration of the Sagrada Família…
but it was the Devil's weather-work
conjuring up a ghost-city
from the last Glacial Maximum,
lost Loonois
gone again in an hour

Praise the Crayfish Christ striding over the waves!
He shrugs on a planet-wide robe of storms
tucks three whales in each pocket
stows Lyonesse under his kelpy arm

Mermaid sightings here
      and there o'er the briny sea
Only one of the sea-maids
      is sister to Alexander the Great
Her dowry? Seven hundred anchors
      no more   no less

Cradle-rocker's Report

The city fell asleep   People couldn't keep their eyes open
Streets and squares   statues and schools   snoozed the days away

I saw no reason to rouse them   as spring rolled on
getting greener and greener   the sea bluer and bluer

Owls flew out hunting in their sleep   the woozy woodpecker
likewise   (not the cuckoo too lazy to lift a wing)

The city slept with the ease of an impresario   Diaghilev or Delfont
It was longer than lifetimes   till the tide of sleep turned

and a dove began the roo-coo roll call
A green linnet scrambled skyward   yelling an important message

A lion roared   left his fresh scat on the President's doorstep
Everyone woke to that familiar whiff   thinking they'd slept no more
                                                than a single night

What a stretchy-stretchy dreamy to-die-for sleep we've had!
How hard we've sucked our thumbs!   Now we're raring to go

Let's plant nine hundred cherry trees   ply the dressmaker with a
                                                million pins
venture towards the happiness   wherever daylight invites us

Prospectus: Lyonesse College

Ornithology and Paper-making
Apple-picking and Engineering
Dancing and Heraldry
Architecture and Rope-walking
Ichthyology and Millinery
Falconry and Shopping
Algebra and Gardening
Dentistry and Fencing
Biology and Book-binding
Geology and Cooking
Photography and Pyrotechnics
Sewing and Apiculture
Archery and Vinoculture
Podiatry and Fortune-telling
Face-booking and Pot-holing
Yachting and Astronomy
Fell-walking and Card-sharping
Athletics and Cider-making
Bibliography and Mountaineering

The Foster Brothers of Kernow Speak

us boys has not
fallen
by green swarths of the hillside
       one beneath another
       in the meads
nor writ the alphabet
with a twig in the sand
nor drowned a crow
in a crucible
nor been allowed
to be wise-lipped
by ladies of Lyonesse
so soft of their pretty skins
       no never

My Old Lover

Fountains were his forte
        my old lover
                water jetting
from the mouths
        of cheerful pewter dolphins
                and morose Neptunes
or spilt from ewers
        toted by stone-blind girls
                He liked all of that
You'd never catch him
        weeping for a year
                like me
hoping for a last glimpse
        of a lover
                in some sea-hued basement bar
or hurrying along
        the quayside
                wanting one last look
or word
        before he and Lyonesse
                vanish forever

Lions on a love prowl

A Lyonesse lion is invisible
on a moonlit silvery shore   so they say

If the beast looks straight at you
everything's fine

If he glances away over his superb shoulder
things are less certain to go well

especially if two more silver lions stroll by
in the company of a maiden lady
bearing the arms of her father –

she cannot display a crest
drawls the first lion   *as she has no helm*

when she marries   remarks the second lion
her husband's arms are united with hers   by impalement

the third lion licks his silvery chops
Oh that carnassial shear, my pet, what a love bite he gives you!

Wooden Lady

Like Thetis
in her briny crypt
she searches
whys and wherefores
searching
for her only friend
in the wake
of the patterny-backed
toddling sea turtle
or in the silence
of the four winds
whose names
are legion
And
that friend?
He'll be
in the last place
she looks

My own volition

I'm paying a flying visit   that's all
nodding to bridges I know by sight
trees in their green habits

In my flight
I find the emerald of astonishment
lost by a road beggar

but a cent's worth of good luck
never comes my way
maybe because I constantly cool my heels
in the lovely past

I'm just visiting,
Lyonesse,
you can't make me stay

Time in the World

There's all the time in the world in *sea-cold* Lyonesse
where the tides rake the gardens to a pebbled Japanese precision

In the city under the sea, time never stands still though you'd bet
your life-savings it did down here in broke-back bird-boned Léonois

The land took the sea on trust   Big mistake
The land gambled with the ocean   Lyonaise rued the day

The sea rolled the land up like an old green carpet
Ocean spun her like a top, made the four winds whistle

The land stayed quiet as a mouse, hoping against hope
But the sea drowned Leonnoys, church by church and field by field
before coming quietly to its own blue heel

So there's all the time in the world
in these sea-cold gardens tide-raked to a Zen precision

Time never stands still in the city under the sea
 where sin-black scabbard fish and dvd-flat ray drift along in a world of
                                their own

with no need for life-savings in bird-boned broke-back Lethowstow
where Jonah emerges cussing from the belly of the whale,

Noah struggles with the bible for the last word
and Lyonesse is no more than graffiti on an invisible wall

Blues

My love's a prince of Lyonesse
a lion he thinks himself
holding absolute sway
singing the Lyonesse blues

He's gravely dear to me
host of my heart
best and worst of men
singing the Lyonesse blues

Get a grip, girlfriend, they said,
or you'll learn them Lyonesse blues

By hook and crook
he comes to me,
loves to hear me croon
those Lyonesse blues

My lover takes his time with me
he takes his time along streets
where the faeries' coachman used to go
singing the Lyonesse blues

Get a life, girlfriend, they said,
or the blues'll grab you
But I was heart-lorn,
hand-fasted to him

and woke in the gutter
singing those Lyonesse blues
as often happens I believe
where love's concerned

My love was a prince
a lion of men I thought him
but death himself stands beside me now
singing the Lyonesse blues

Solo

Get thee behind me
Lyonesse

don't ask me
any more wise
and wondrous questions

Dear to me are my fears
and my firefly tears

Don't wipe them away
with your hindsight hand

Who's down there

    at the bottom o' the sea

        drinking 'is fill o' Doom Bar?

            Davy, Davy, tis thee?

Sermon of the Crayfish Christ, or The Latitudes

Blessed are they who live on their wits, Beloveds, for they shall see further than the Lookouts on the cliff.

Blessed are the pure in heart, for they shall be spared the butchering platform.

Blessed are those who sail the *Persistencia* around the globe for a thousand years, for they will inherit the Arctic Ocean, the North Atlantic, the South Atlantic, the Indian Ocean, the North Pacific, the South Pacific and even the Antarctic Ocean, yea, verily, the Seven Seas.

> *Congregation sings:*
>
> *Go down you pinks and posies*
> *Go down you blood red roses*
> *Go down where them whalefish blow*

Blessed are the merciful, for they shall be saved even when crossing the Kraken Mare, *the hollow oak your palace be...*

Blessed are the Adventurous, for they shall be given Adventure.

Blessed be thou, Hazardous reef where a hundred ships have foundered, for the Ocean will comfort thee.

> *Congregation sings:*
>
> *Go down you pinks and posies*
> *Go down you blood red roses*
> *Go down where them whalefish blow*

Blessed are they that are press-ganged for my Name's Sake, for I will give you the winds tied up in a handkerchief and no ship you grace will ever sink.

Blessed art thou, Mary Ellen, don't look so glum, a couple more hymns and you'll be drinking hot rum.

Blessed are they that have lost everything, for theirs is the Kingdom of Lyonesse way down where them whalefish blow…

Rejoice and be glad   and be exceeding glad!
Here endeth   Here endeth   Here endeth   Here endeth

When and If

you write about Lyonesse
write in silver ink on scarlet parchment

describe lions and sea-gardens
but never mention

the life of Christ
His all-seeing eyes are blind to Lyonesse

If and when
you draw a map of our metropolis

include every sundial and boulevard
paint the circling city walls bright

as a marriage belt woven of ten colour-silks
two more than the rainbow for Lethowsow

When and if
you record the day the Fool of Leonnoyes

heard a golden Lion roar a warning
every hour on the hour

Fool who watched the city slip under the wave
but never said a word

tell that to the credulous world
straight from the water-horse's gob

Blessing

Matthew Mark Luke and John
bless the bed that I lie on
Under waves of blue and green
under tides so quiet and stern

Bless the day that I was born
Bless the day of Sturm und Drang
Bless the sea floor I lie on
Bless Lyonesse who lost the sun

Matthew Mark Luke and John
bless the bed that I lie on
bless the waves of blue and green
bless the tides so quiet and stern

Goodbye

Perhaps they loved their city too well
bells steeples and all
and feared the sea too little
Perhaps like Shakespeare's faeries
those *thieves of time*
they were blown away on the west wind
sunbeam by sunbeam

Or perhaps like those fays
that since have broke their gifted wands
Lyonesse broke herself
did a runner
taking her sorcerer's leave
with a trace of wave-sparkle
a hint of job done...

Lyonesse
full of grace
and no looking back

NOTES

21: 'The Gownshops': *water-lions of the west*: from 'Sea Unicorns and Land Unicorns' by Marianne Moore.

22: 'Our Cradle Sea': quotation from *The Anathemata* by David Jones. *lully lullay*: phrase from an old English lullaby carol.

23: *'Strike, strike the bell'*: Title of traditional sea shanty.

24: 'Make a Wish': *The Ship's Last Sigh* is the name of a memorial sculpture by Amandus Heinrich Adamson, Estonian sculptor and painter, in remembrance of the Russian ship *Rusalka*, lost with all hands in the Gulf of Finland, 1893.

28: 'Sentimental Customs': *Will you be my valentine?*: Originally, Victorian custom: phrase used on Valentine's Day to ask someone if they want to spend the day together and exchange gifts.

30: *'by the hoar rock in the drowned wood'*: quotation from *The Anathemata*, David Jones.

31: *in the sullen courts of sleep* and *roofs, walls, belfries of the foundered town*: 'Sunk Lyonesse' by Walter de la Mare.

32: SS *Blue Jacket*: wrecked on a clear night off Lands End, November 1898.

33: 'Legends': *lewyon*: lions (Cornish).

35: 'Owls': The Wolf is the single-rock Wolf Lighthouse off the south-west coast of Cornwall, so called because the fissures in the rock produce a howling sound in gales.

36: *'clad me naked'*: from 'The Lay of Havelok the Dane'. The phrase 'belongs to a class of tags which cover all sorts of meanings by the coupling of two adjectives of opposite meanings': from the notes to lines 987-1338 by the Reverend Walter W Skeat (revised second edition by K. Sisam, 1915).

39: 'My Friend': *casement and porch* and *green translucency*: from 'Sunk Lyonesse' by Walter de la Mare. An *ope* (or *opeway*) is a Cornish vernacular term for a town or village alleyway leading down to the sea.

42: The Devil's Seam is the garboard seam of a ship. In the

old days it had to be sealed with hot pitch, therefore it was termed a devil of a job.

44: 'Lizzie': Lizzie Siddal, mistress, then wife, of Dante Gabriel Rossetti.

46: 'Holy Father Lions': 'scientific sonar'. See 'Lyonesse Project' for details of continuing sidescan sonor investigations into possible location of a sunken city off the coastline of the Isles of Scilly: www.cismas.org.uk/lyonesse.php

47: 'O Shake That Girl with the Blue Dress On': song title. 'partner in fainting': Peter Redgrove (unpublished notebook).

49: 'Rusalka': a water sprite, from the opera of the same name by Antonín Dvořák. See also the sinking of the Russian ship, *Rusalka* (note to page 24).

52: 'Sewing Lesson under the Sea': *Birds-in-the-air. Wind-blown Square*: traditional patchwork quilt patterns.

59: '*Up jumps the shark*': 'Holy Ground': area of a sea-port where working girls plied their trade (original reference from a sea shanty set in the city of Cork).

60: 'Starlit': *put 'im in the long boat / put 'er in the long boat*: adapted from traditional sea shanty.

62: '*Many brave hearts are asleep in the deep, so beware, beware*': traditional sea shanty.

64: 'Twinned with Canopus': Canopus, an ancient submerged Egyptian city, recently excavated. *What fools these mortals be…*: Shakespeare, *A Midsummer Night's Dream*.

65: '*They say the voiced angel is an invention of the English*': Quotation from early English text, relating to choral music.

66: '*More deadly than the Siren's song is the Siren's silence*': In Greek mythology, the Sirens were dangerous female entities who sat on rocky islands and lured nearby sailors to shipwreck with their enchanting singing. See also: Franz Kafka, *The Silence of the Sirens*: 'Now the Sirens have a still more fatal weapon than their song, namely their silence. And though admittedly such a thing has never happened, still it is conceivable that someone might possibly have escaped from their singing; but from their silence certainly never.'

66: Mrs Do-As-You-Would-Be-Done-By is a sub-aqua character in *The Water Babies*, a novel by Charles Kingsley, 1863.

71: 'The Devil': *all the ruthless architectural audacity...* from a guidebook to the Sagrada Família, Barcelona.

78: 'Lions on a love prowl': 'carnassial shear': term for a lion's bite, which is a sideways-gnawing action whereby the lion shears off slices of the flesh of its prey.

79: 'Wooden Lady': term for a ship's figurehead shaped like a woman's head and shoulders.

85: 'Who's down there': Doom Bar is a popular Cornish ale.

86: 'Sermon of the Crayfish Christ, or The Latitudes': *Go down you pinks and posies... down where them whalefish blow* and *Blessed art thou, Mary Ellen...*: These quotations are from traditional sea shanties.

90: 'Goodbye': *thieves of time... sunbeam by sunbeam... that since have broke their gifted wands...* I found the above fragments jotted down in my notebook but have been unable to trace their provenance.

*

In a footnote in *The Anathemata*, David Jones writes of 'the identification of the Leonnoys or Lyonesse of Romance literature with the sea-area beyond Land's End; and the independent native Cornish tradition of the submergence of a countryside with the loss of one hundred and forty churches in that area...' and he records that 'the disputed theory that an old Cornish compound word meaning "the hoar rock in the wood" is an authentic pre-inundation site-name for the rocky island now called St Michael's Mount.'

Lyonesse is also known by these variant French, Breton and Cornish names: Leonnoys, Léonois, Loonois, Lethostow, Lyonaise.

Lyonesse began in a workshop run by Katrina Naomi in Cornwall in January 2015. Katrina gave each of us an individual theme. Mine was 'to write about a city'. But I had just written a number of poems about London, and a couple about Bristol. I felt citied-out. I went into the gardens, wandered about in the Cornish drizzle. I had no idea what to write about. Suddenly a line popped into my head out of nowhere – 'The gownshops of Lyonnese took satin for granted...' The first rough draft of the first Lyonesse poem then followed.

I owe Katrina Naomi a great debt, firstly for sparking off these poems, and secondly for her scrupulous close-reading of the manuscript in progress.

I am indebted to John Greening for an early reading of some of these poems, for key comments, and for a borrowed phrase. My thanks to Kay Cotton, for the suggestion of 'The Latitudes' for part of the title of the Crayfish Christ sermon poem. I am as ever grateful to the members of Falmouth Poetry Group for their valued comments. My thanks to Sylvia Miles for additional proof-reading.

NEW LAMPS FOR OLD

cup of evenings

the house
is running on empty
the rooms sigh
for something
someone
anyone

let's go out
and walk the evening
all the way down to the sea

we won't trust the boat captain
or his bullhorn

you can tell me
owls are the only birds
capable of seeing the colour blue

that after you die
you will not mind anything

shall we go out
into the long-ago summer evening
you my dear Duke Orsino
me my usual self

and drink our fill of the evening
as we always did
from Falmouth held out to us
applewood cup filled to the brim?

what is the air made of?

those rooms
you like to live in
are drawn on air

their doors
their leaning towers

deeper than the well
of the world
is this hour of rooms
sketched on the air

never was there such an hour

new lamps for old

sang the harp

prepare for sorrow
and silence

for sleeping alone
on the bare floor

new lamps for old
sang the harp

learn to eat alone
in the cold kitchen

to walk golden cliff
and sunlit tide line alone

get used to the hard work
of it   sang the harp

silver spoon
in time's mouth

new lamps for old

husband

of the quarries and dug-outs of the sea
      husband of the sleep-tight tide
husband near the bare hedge
      where the wild ponies feel the pinch
husband of winter rain on the holly and the ivy
      trails through old woods
husband of all he surveys
      a thousand footsteps in the empty house
husband of the greenways and cliffs
      of the western ocean   our playground
husband of fancy-dress clouds by night
      and stars shining down as if they cared
husband of the open book
      stone page where the world ends

home

getting you home
all in one piece
is a work in progress
but let's not despair
every anthill
every eagle is on our side
don't take no for an answer
say the hills
hurry up
says the tortoise
when at last I get you home
be it on the Feast Day of St Philibert
or next Wednesday
we'll walk through the rainy orchard
aisles of apple trees
on the brink of apple-drop
and never ask
who forgives? who forgets?

Dusk coming on

Tregarthen, November

Old granite boulders draw in their Penwith horns,
saddle rock, stone in the pool of water,
stone with the furze bush,
stone west of the hole bridge.
The horizon's drawn in blue and pink
as by a map-maker's unerring hand.
Above roofless chapel and muddy spring
jackdaws squabble and recce a roost.
Here's a church of the twilight hours
gone wild in the wooded vale,
its lintel split and thrawn
with ivy and hawthorn.
Dwarfish elder hunkers down.
A step away, the watch hills, no stars yet...

sevenfold

leafy pavements
where I walk to school
long after evensong
in days
before these days

sun-shivers along rookery road
always autumn
tree roots knuckling
through broken tarmac
lifetimes ago

the freight train
tows away
fifteen empty sandpit-yellow wagons

fly-by-night

only the moon abroad in her finery
saw the lost one go
down where the valley brims with hawthorn

came so close   the lost
but slipped away   star-ripple in the river

fly-by-night   fly-by-night
even the power station puts away its work
how sad to be in this immense world now

some strange hour of night

all of night's dark
fits exactly
into the silence of a few stars

books sleep their stories
rooms flicker
from churchtown to churchtown

this hour of night goes by
for me alone
it seems

hour no one will remember for me
no one helping no one hindering

hour shaped like a spoon of the Celts
or a sword they offered
most cherished   to flowing water

strangest of hours   no lamp can light for me

Swarthmoor Hall, Ulverston

after two days of sun
and cloudlessness
today is all brinks –
brink of rain
brink of solstice
brink of silence and solitude

in this prayerful garden
I'm on the brink
of I don't know what –
I'm waiting
for something to begin
rain or thought or deed
I don't mind

*

rain comes
       out of nowhere –
an old wall runs quickly
       round
       the garden where
summer lives
       by leaf by flower
       the rain comes
taking me
under its wing

*

pleach the hornbeam hedge
in the Quiet Garden
prune the appletrees
seal their wounds with wax

      soldier alliums
      in their purple busbies
      sway in the breeze

      the bee doubts no one and nothing

*

carry a handful of ash
from the fire pit

scatter it in the beck flowing
between shadow and sunlight
under the oaks

seal wounds with love
prune hedge and apple tree
follow each wound
seal it with wax

a jot of blossom falls
on the flat roof of the hive
from a tall old may tree

*

any one of us has wounds
          waiting to be sealed
as a pruned tree or quick hedge
          has its hurt sealed with wax

*

on a solstice morning
veiling everything in cloudy heat
I let green steep into me
and all the gardens lost in me

a morning flirting with storm
summer on the back foot
hills beyond hunching away
the inland lighthouse
standing on its dignity

*

slow clouds sleeping their way
across the sky
bonny with light   not rain
clouds full of hidden sun
(where's their flock-master?)

*

every leaf unfurled
full of witness to green to summer's lease
old walls hold the heat   loosely
between one minute and the next
as bees sink or swim   from flower to flower
a swarm of bees   a silver spoon

above the fell   clouds slip and slide for miles

*

they're here again
the midsummer dead

the sun brings them
out of hiding

here they are
they take up little room

millions of them together
no heavier than a blade of grass

some in a state of grace
some who'll never know where or who they are

drifting back into view
on the longest day of the year

remembered   unremembered

*

a cloud and another cloud   skim slowly by
as if they know   what no one knows
as if sealing wounds   one by one
could be done   by a cloud or anyone

*

a gabble of finches
from the silver birch

a mesmerism of blackbirds
in the big oaks

*

he has a lovely thinking song
the blackbird in the silver birch

his notes come wild and true
then he's silent till he calls again

he's hidden in those shivery leaves
singing as a healing wound sings

his here-and-gone song
scuds on the breeze towards the beck

and though just as lovely
grows less adjacent to me

and so I let it go

*

crow-song shoves up
raw and needy from the meadows

I know his game in the rooky wood

*

by the side of the Hall
I went along a narrow path
stony enough for Mister Pilgrim

across the meadow
I saw two crows on the wall
an elder and a fledgling

keeping so still and watchful
I learned they were two hawks
a fledgling and an elder

*

things decide to continue
dry stone walls   the fells
garden blackbirds   crows and finches
the beck   the summer oaks
the hills   all the flowers known and unknown to me
every blade of grass   all decide to continue

*

a bee grunts his way   from flower to flower
red rose of Lancaster   white rose of York

not enough butterflies   to go round
wisdom also   on the wane

big green-veined leaves   shaped like hearts
others like   big listening ears

fire pit and wheelbarrow   that bee drones back to the hive
clouds overhead   are high-strung with rain

the silver birch quivers for rain   but the clouds are giving nothing
away

*

the owl sighs across the little night
the beck runs quiet under the oaks

*

rose and allium
crane's bill and cornflower
oak
silver birch and sycamore
in step
with the rain

honeysuckle and meadow grass
plum tree   and beck
that row of oaks   swaying their upper branches
orchard   and flower beds
                  all dizzy with rain
small dark yews   sopping-wet and shining

even the stones in the drystone wall
open quartz mouths and drink

*

oaks and yew trees
are rain aviaries –
a flit
a glimpse
a couple of sung notes
then back into bird-hiding

rain is the day's rule of thumb
measuring the hours
filling the cisterns
briefly slackening
before renewing its vow –

to fall from on high
like this
          like this
                    like this

*

next day
  grey sky garden
    chill air
no rain
  unseen birds pitching quiet notes
            clandestine:
garden paths of Swarthmoor
  turning back
      on themselves
  as I peer
      through branches
to unknown months ahead

my house

quiet rain
on the window
of a quiet bedroom
where first light
gathers its thoughts
where the floor
remembers
and the door
knows its place
rain pulling the strings
fooling no one
raindrops
tip-toppling
into an empty milk bottle
on the old doorstep
quiet listening hard
to nothing and no one

St Olave's Church

Tooley Street, London

Your prayers have nowhere to go
along Tooley Street
nor can you take refuge from your troubles
in St Olave's churchyard
by the river by London Bridge
always was a chilly foggy place anyhow
They pulled it down in 1926
brick by dirty brick
church and vestry hall
The tower gathered its wits
took itself off sadly and wisely
to Tanner Street Gardens
to live a new life as a forlorn remnant
and on the site of the church you'll now find St Olaf House,
a building that's almost changed its sex
by making full use of this *most valuable and useful piece of waterfront*
No sign of that devout dingy old hulk
except   now and then
you find your prayer
taking you along Tooley Street
where an altar hangs invisibly about
evensong hums silently to itself
the shade of Henry Gauntlett saunters by
and St Olave-by-the-Bridge knows what you're thinking
and why a prayer is all you've got to show for

Village of La Baleine

In this green and rivery region
you'll find not a single whale,
a trout farm is the closest you'll come,
tucked-in a step beyond
the smokery...
No one knows where the whale is,
in English or French.
Did someone once dream
a whale swam up-river?

Isn't it a pleasant thing
that this auberge is called *Le Krill*?
Perhaps from a mile up in the sky
there's a whale-shaped hill
to be seen? The whale-name's
a puzzle but not an urgent one...
Let's turn our attention to these chic purple orchids,
those clouds of hedgerow dandelions
and (quelle surprise) to a laggard band
of Tour de France cyclists in ladybird-bright lycra,
havering at a crossroads where two signposts
point their arrows in opposite directions,
both reading, *La Baleine*.

Normandy

as long as the thorn tree stands

faint traces   in the grass   a fragmentary long room
and a creep passage   west of the house
two small oval chambers   reminiscent of beehives
shadows of feast rooms   shifting in wind and rain
hidden trackways   across old moorland
rune-carved milestones   ghost ditches   shadow sites
soil-marks   airborne remote sensing of scanty chapels
a scatter of portable altars   crop marks in the plough-soil
a medieval garden   tucked into the lee of an earth bank
where a man or woman sometimes appears   and disappears
one of many portals   where anyone might be imprisoned
like True Thomas   wandering the elf-lands
till he forgets   how to tell a lie

Kandinsky at the Tate

(for Zoe)

Years ago we're swimming through Kandinsky,
hundreds of us,
some doggy-paddling by,
others employing a sedate thoughtful breast-stroke.
A few fast-laners power along at Olympic speed,
snapping heads sideways for a good gulp of painted air.
I'm treading water, you're pearl-diving,
holding your breath for a closer deeper look.
Tate lifeguards sit on high black observation stools,
each with a long invisible pole
in readiness
to fish out those drowning in colours,
for there are always those who go out of their depth,
over-estimating stamina, getting cramps…
Panicky splashing! but rescue is swiftly accomplished,
the Kandinsky-fied one given the kiss of life…
as you and I float gently out into the thirty-two boroughs.

Hell

The hospital corridors go in straight lines,
make sharp left and right turns,
but I'm not fooled, this place is one of the circles of hell.
If with better words, better magic,
I could've made you rise from your bed
in the HDU and led you away, I'd have done it.
But I couldn't. Three years later, here
for a minor out-patient procedure,
I enter by the same dreadful *Porte d'Enfer*
through which the paramedics brought you,
confused and combative... I run the gauntlet of reception,
walk swiftly past the stair that leads to the renal unit,
soft-lit despairing ward with its useless machinery
of revival where you were finally lodged...
Along the corridors I mingle with a host
of bandaged medicated frame-walking or chair-bound damned,
and the damned who come to visit,
never knowing what they'll find, parents, siblings, lovers,
spouses changed beyond recognition,
hoping-against-hope visitants
who must return home, that further circle of hell,
silenced rooms and prayer-less thoughts,
what are we to do there?

longing is part of it

and shame
and a pinch of quietest doubt
fear is part of it and dream
dreaming especially is an important part
judgement and care
are part of it
as are fury and pain and despair
everything is part of it
even the lovely light of early morning
showing you its heavy heart and its woe
I used to go to Halloween all the time but now I stay indoors

the train is

leaving has left
that I haven't boarded
the journey is beginning
that I haven't begun
haven't begun because of the rain
because of the sad
because of the bullet-dreamy brain
the train has left is leaving again
on its way through the counties of rain
and I'm not onboard the train
as it sighs and putters along the line
no I'm still here
in the cloudy attic
packing and unpacking
in the roof's floating world
yes the train leaving has left
without me to say which way it must go
turn left at Plymouth
then grouch all the way to London
the train that's gone and left me here
and no one saw me go

Ruby Loftus screwing a breech ring for a Bofors Anti-Aircraft Gun

(after the painting by Laura Knight, 1943)

green hairnet
red blouse
blue dungarees
this former tobacconist's assistant
no more than twenty-one
girl from a back street
pencilled eyebrows
lots of scarlet lippy
rolled-up sleeves
stands at her workbench
in command
of a huge clattering machine
its callipers, spanners, blocks
the tools of the trade

it usually takes eight years
to train for this task
Ruby mastered it
in as many weeks
her hands
covered in oil
but steady at the lathe
virginal gun-maker at her work of ordnance

break of day/this one evening

sequent lit windows
of the first train
ambling by
to the docks

soft click
of the central heating

> *linnets nest*
> *and breed*
> *in forty-four countries*
> *from Andorra*
> *to Ukraine*

the radio voice goes
in one ear
and out the other

it does not say
your numbered days
are over
though it is a fact,
it is true

*

fragments of summer 1976
out-of-the-blue Boscastle kisses
the sea casting its blue net wide

imagine living without sorrow
I'd forgotten life used to be like that

lovely carefree summers
like old palaces overgrown with wild roses
drift of petals on a wooden floor

*

my thought
wanders away
like a Rossini aria
written long ago
but never sung

Auntie Wavelette's
forty-seven
beloved scarves
tucked in the coffin
going up in flames with her

*

a hummingbird-hawkmoth
butts the window
by which I'm reading
scaring me
but only for a second
with its thwarted passion
for the light

I bundle it
in the curtain
shake it out into midnight air,
husky wings
of the creature beating
fast and furious
as it goes

*

spread the years out
a fan to tell fortunes

far away
tall stone pillars
throw shadows
on a chequered floor
and
wild wheat grows
in the sand

crystals are forming
straight masses of orthite

someone picks a rose
ten years too late

glance

I glance over my shoulder
there you are
no I haven't forgotten you
but my life's
had other things to do
years and days lost at sea
the silver salty snappy sea
and to this day
I haven't learned how to love
    holy fool heart
    I hear you say
    may you learn better one day
as you fade away
gleam by gleam
like a small lovely morning
only you and I can see
and now it's gone

other elements

I can't say *my life* any more
instead I say
the sun took me along the way
in an air from The Orient
(I was taken)

I won't say *my life*
is like this or like that
I leave it to its fate
the sprite of the moment
putting its mark on me
never to be shifted

our days of life
were days I remember and forget
a hundred times a day,
old radio tunes
heard in the foreign street

those days came and went
I loved them so
If you think you're forgotten,
days,
think again,
that day has yet to dawn

love letters

No, no, let me –
I am tying the old wizard's tie

Wystan's half-man, half-tree,
talking up his best leaves

and his love letters
and his weather behind with the rent

I don't care about the Honours List!

His eyes blaze
like the entire Solar System squeezed
into my bedroom

Look out, Auden's about!

May time

is hospital visits,
fear, sadness, fury,
a surplus of light, needle-
sharp, the now
of now, the so of what.
May is when hope
needs a visa
to enter the country
and where's that coming from
when finding a parking space
at the hospital
takes every ounce of courage?
Back home
I pull on the dunce-cap
of sleep, then
up jumps
another bright as a beehive
morning, light hitting
all the nails on their poor heads,
the drive to the hospital,
fury, sadness, fear,
grimness, reaping.

Ann Boleyn's Music Book

(for Sylvia Miles)

Maid of honours, her book has forty-two songs
writ in an English hand, but not her final singing.
  O Death rock me asleep

I will give you pleasure dear sang Ann
perhaps to more than one man, perhaps not.
  O Death rock me asleep

Mistresse A Bolleyne loved de Sermisy
and Josquin, love songs and prayers.
  O Death rock me asleep

Flirt's scrapbook for singing the hours
or a scholar's Missa plurium modulorum?
  O Death rock me asleep

Lute and harp, falcon and pomegranate.
Jouyssance vous donneray, she sang.
  O Death rock me asleep

May evening

white cows
shimmying slowly
through the deep-grass grazing valley
under a bright half-moon
in the last half hour of light,
the sky falling bluer and bluer
by the minute
into dusk
      a field away
the pigs loosed *de herbagio*

Under Ragged Stone Hill

Under the hill
everything's supplied,
you don't have to bring a thing,
all's here for the asking,
oodles of irony
and jollity
in the oak tree college
where a jackdaw
is a crow
but a crow is not a jackdaw
Can you hear
that squeaky metallic evensong
blaring from their green
and gleaming throats
chyak-chyak-chyak amen?
      I think you can

*

Under the hill
there is always the rain

but on the other hand
there is always the rain

Rain for the jackerdaws,
rain on their silvery heads

Rain for the white stump-oak
and the nettle-barn

Rain for the smallest of crows
rain for the so-called sea-crow

*

The leaves so green
need no one's permission
to move in the breeze

The stones in the field
so wise
need no jackdaw-permission
to think their deep thoughts

The grass
grown tall and random
can please itself
about growing another inch a day

and the field-hedge,
with its responsibilities as border
and boundary,

takes no shit from anyone,
not even the western jackdaw,
squares off the world neat and trim

*

If you and yours
are jackerdaws,
brisk upright *Corvus monedula*,
there is tree-top life-style
and hop-on-the-fence
like a big ole flea,
there's scoop-down on gnat-rich cowpat
and berry-bush forage,
there's sky research,
rain-pluck in the wing,
sun's single upright moment,
and this most voluble of birds
telling everything slant
under Ragged Stone Hill
(if you and yours are daws)

*

Under Ragged Stone Hill
we chawks drink from the mist
and the cattle-trod stream
We seek out the seed on stony ground
as is our biblical fashion,
are loud as muck across the field edge –
under Ragged Stone Hill we make our name

*

where there are rags
you will find riches
say the daws

where there are stones
you will find stones
say the daws

the swans will sing
when the jackdaws are silent
say the Greeks

*

I'm at the foot of the hill
with the cows and the daws and the flies

Over beyond
Tom and Harry are dismantling

the yellow tractor
diagnosing faults as they go

The daws belt out their calling flight,
the cattle doze

Two weeks past midsummer
the year's clock ticks on

in green-leaf, dust and sudden rain,
first hydrangea, last foxglove

*

The year's clock-hands are mist and sun,
they go round,
big hand and little hand

Daws are black minutes
shadowing green hours of day

Mist takes the hill by surprise
dissolving the hours
so the half-moon can rise again
yellow as butter
on the child's first-ever slice of bread

*

Primacy of daws
is how it goes
under Ragged Stone Hill
despite the badger's quilly visits,
despite the here there gone of deer,
cautious rabbit and foolhardy hare,
cows ganging up on the sleepy bull

But: *primacy* of daws, any daw will tell you,
is how it goes here under Ragged Stone Hill

*

They're still here!
Jack-crows in the cow meadows since
great-grandfather's day!
The farmer's wife points and shrugs

Before the ancestors,
before the farm and the cows –
jackdaws
in the fields under the hill

*

The farmhouse is timbered
like an old ship of Tudor times,
beams gouged from oaks
buffeted by storms,
their mappy swirls and hatchments
telling my hand – trust, touch, travel me,
I nested many a daw,
sailed my crows-nest seas

*

Meanwhile,
        outside –
the trees
        playing living statues,
the hill ducking its head
        as the crow flies

*

The holly bush has no heart,
says a daw

The holly bush has no common-sense,
says another daw

The holly bush has no philosophy,
says a third

The holy holly bush looks fine to me,
I say

Three jackerdaws line up,
make eye-contact,

pity me my innocence,
offer a beak-load of advice

*

Jack moon over hill and holly bush
over ragged stone and bumble-sheep
Jack moon yellow moon come-back-soon moon

*

A jackdaw never wears a wristwatch
I slip the battery from the back of the clock
Once upon a time, observes a daw,
that's all you need to know

*

This morning
the mildest possible light
swings the hill round,
the milky sky is here to help the dawn,
adding extra tranquillity,
scoop by scoop,
to the green oaks circling the hill-foot,
making everything look magical,
a lost forest of child-time,
where only the jackerdaw is permitted to fly home

clouds in the sky

it was late but not too late
there were some clouds in the sky
and a bitch-unicorn trotting by

it was early but not too early
there were rivers
and blue farms, like things out of a painting

the hour was milky as a little Dorset dairy
no one knew why
neither Van Gogh nor Seurat

it was early and it was late
the timber wolf grinned into the camera
hoping David Attenborough was watching him

wild rose

or prick-rose
in her heyday
trusting no one
with any of her nine lives
wild rose smites the air
with a spicery or two
rose is afterwards
is wise only when sleeping
has canker-craft
and selfhood of petal
she's a scrambler
the very reason of rain
in royal realms as far as you can see
her nature is where and when
footnote among thistle-beds

Malvern Link

Malvern Link roses   reds deep
as the brickwork of the bridge
summer dusts and rains them   new houses
surround the rectangle of the town cemetery
the hills roll along   dear Malvern green and cloudy above
as the train pines away with us
I count harvest bales   in shiny black wrap
red kites storm-rich farmsteads
dear Malvern   as we skimmer away
otter-brown river   then the ugliest building in Worcester
new   tin-cheap   blunt   shameful   sun-gilded
and into Worcester Foregate Street where once I waited
for a train to Ledbury that never came   *cancelled cancelled cancelled*
Now May Hill there you are
last-glimpse blue of your green green of your blue
seen and gone   sun on the tips of your big cousins The Malverns
you vanish away too fast beyond orchard after orchard
worldly   with a full bearing of apples

the four queens find Lancelot sleeping

sleep lasts half a minute
or twelve days
sleep's the gift of lofty mountains
or not
the river's nod
every freshet and brook
sleep chucks herself down a well
sleep's the cursive hooks
and hinges
of a love letter
set to music
on Fridays and Saturdays
sleep keeps the radio on
all night
bits of Schumann
Blossom Dearie
The Troggs   Dowland
sleep lasts five minutes
or nine years   you know this

found poem: **Swarthmoor Hall**

two vizard masks
for my sister Rachel
and for my selfe

a wooden writing box

a bed made of lignum vitae
the heaviest wood in the world

eighteen yards
of blacke and sky-coulered ribbin

two scarlet petticoats
to be carried to Kendal

new petticoats
of blacke and of dove couler

wooden crib
with butterfly-motif quilt

painted clover-box
for carriage of ye clover,
grasse seeds of Lancashire

crib with six knobs
for cat netting

shotte to keep crowes
off the wheate

sword chest
painted the green
of Lady Jane Grey's eyes

Three Years

In 2001
someone or something
added an hour
to the stairs, Peter.
In 2002
the same busybody
moved the town
out of your reach,
along with the coastal path,
and The Lizard.
By summer 2003
you had no further use
for any of these,
so you gave them back,
as good as you'd found them.

In the mirror

there are mountains and rivers
and the curve of the earth
as it travels the void,
quiet towns, endless
gardens. The mirror is smaller
than a tear. Cities are visible,
islands and ruined places.
Pericles, oceans and storms.
The burning cores of steel mills.
Lower Marsh with the centuries
on his back. Warehouses
at St Katherine's Dock
brimming with ivy. The mirror,
smaller than a tear or the curve
of the earth.

NOTES

105: 'sevenfold': The Holy Spirit is one in name, but sevenfold in virtues.

108: 'Swarthmoor Hall, Ulverston': a mansion near Ulverston, known as 'the cradle of Quakerism'. This sequence of poems was written while I was on retreat at Swarthmoor Hall in 2014.

118: 'St Olave's Church': The last church of this name was built in 1743 on the eastern side of the southern edge of London Bridge, and demolished in 1926. Henry Gauntlett was organist at the church from 1827 to 1846. The church was dedicated to Olav Haraldsson, an early King of Norway, who attempted to convert his people to Christianity and was martyred in 1030. Olav became a popular saint in England, and five churches in the City of London were dedicated to him, apart from the church at Southwark. A memorial plaque can be seen on St Olaf House, opposite the entrance to London Bridge Station.

121: 'Kandinsky at the Tate': This poem was written after visiting the Kandinsky Exhibition at Tate Modern in 2008.

125: 'Ruby Loftus screwing a breech ring for a Bofors Anti-Aircraft Gun': Dame Laura Knight painted Ruby at work in The Royal Ordnance Factory, Newport, South Wales in 1943.

135: 'Under Ragged Stone Hill': This was written while staying at White House Farm, Hollybush, Worcestershire, in July 2019.

145: 'Malvern Link': A train station near Ledbury. This poem was written after a visit to Ledbury Poetry Festival.

146: *'the four queens find Lancelot sleeping'*: a sketch by David Jones.